VOICES OF INSPIRATION

Timeless Wisdom from History's Greatest Minds

MOSES FEEHI

Acknowledgments

I would like to express my deepest gratitude to all the extraordinary minds whose words have graced the pages of this book. The quotes and insights from leaders, philosophers, scientists, artists, and visionaries have inspired countless individuals throughout history, and it is their timeless wisdom that continues to shape and uplift us today.

This book would not exist without the profound contributions of figures such as Jesus Christ, Mahatma Gandhi, Martin Luther King Jr., Albert Einstein, Eleanor Roosevelt, Nelson Mandela, Mother Teresa, Winston Churchill, and many others. Their words transcend time and culture, offering guidance, hope, and strength to those who seek to grow and better themselves.

I also extend heartfelt thanks to the numerous historical and modern thinkers who are not directly quoted but whose legacies have paved the way for future generations. Their enduring impact continues to resonate, reminding us that wisdom, compassion, and perseverance are the foundations of meaningful success.

To the readers: May the words within these pages offer you inspiration and insight as you journey through life, just as they have for so many before you. Let their wisdom serve as a beacon of light, guiding you toward personal growth, success, and fulfillment.

Contents

INTRODUCTION

Why "Voices of Inspiration?"

Inspiration is the invisible force that drives us forward. It helps us push through adversity, set our sights higher, and find strength in the face of challenges. Throughout history, humanity has been shaped by the words and wisdom of those who dared to think beyond the ordinary, lead with purpose, and spark change in the world. These voices—sometimes echoing across centuries, other times shaping the world we live in today—are more than just words. They are powerful reflections of the minds and hearts that have transformed societies, industries, and individuals.

"Voices of Inspiration" was born from the desire to capture this timeless wisdom in a form that resonates deeply with the modern reader. In our fast-paced world, we often seek quick motivation or guidance, something to remind us of our potential, our ability to persevere, or the importance of kindness. What better way to fuel our journeys than by drawing upon the experiences and insights of the greatest thinkers, leaders, and innovators in human history?

This book compiles **365 quotes**—one for every day of the year—so that every single day, you can turn a page and find a spark of inspiration. Whether you're searching for words of wisdom on perseverance, leadership, courage, or success, the voices included here offer guidance that transcends time, culture, and discipline.

From the philosophical reflections of ancient thinkers like Aristotle and Confucius to the powerful words of modern icons like Nelson Mandela and Maya Angelou, this collection celebrates the diversity of human thought. It brings together leaders, artists, scientists, and visionaries who, in their own ways, have helped shape the world through their ideas, actions, and resilience.

This is more than a book of quotes. **"Voices of Inspiration"** is a resource you can turn to for strength and encouragement. It is a guide through the ups and downs of life, a reminder that the challenges you face today have been faced and overcome by others before you. Their words are a testament to the enduring human spirit and the power of ideas to inspire greatness in all of us.

In these pages, you'll find wisdom that speaks to every part of the human experience: the joy of success, the strength found in failure, the importance of compassion, and the courage to stand up for what is right. These are the voices that have shaped history, and their echoes still inspire us today.

As you embark on this journey of daily inspiration, take a moment to reflect on each quote. How does it speak to you? How can you apply its message to your life? In doing so, you'll find that the voices in this book are not just reminders of past greatness—

they are calls to action, inviting you to contribute your own voice to the ongoing narrative of human progress.

This collection is meant to inspire, guide, and encourage you to live with purpose and to strive for excellence in all that you do. Let these voices remind you that, no matter the circumstances, there is always wisdom to be found, and inspiration waiting to be uncovered.

Welcome to **"Voices of Inspiration"**—your daily companion for discovering the wisdom and greatness within yourself.

1. THE POWER OF PERSEVERANCE

Perseverance is the force that fuels progress. It is the unwavering determination to keep moving forward, despite the obstacles and setbacks that inevitably come our way. The path to success is rarely straight, and history has shown us time and again that those who achieve greatness are not necessarily the most talented or the luckiest, but the ones who refuse to give up. Perseverance is the key to unlocking potential, pushing beyond limits, and achieving what once seemed impossible.

This chapter brings together the voices of leaders, thinkers, and creators who have understood the value of resilience. These 60 quotes serve as reminders that perseverance is not just about enduring hardship—it's about facing adversity with the belief that every challenge is an opportunity to grow stronger. The power of perseverance lies in its ability to transform obstacles into stepping stones toward success.

Let these quotes inspire you to keep pushing forward, no matter what obstacles you face, and remember: progress is made by taking one step at a time, no matter how small that step may seem.

1.

"It does not matter how slowly you go as long as you do not stop."

— Confucius

2.

"Perseverance is failing 19 times and succeeding the 20th."

— Julie Andrews

3.

"The only way to achieve the impossible is to believe it is possible."

— Charles Kingsleigh

4.

"Many of life's failures are people who did not realize how close they were to success when they gave up."

— Thomas Edison

5.

"Success is not final, failure is not fatal: It is the courage to continue that counts."

— Winston Churchill

6.

"The greatest glory in living lies not in never falling, but in rising every time we fall."

— Nelson Mandela

7.

"Courage doesn't always roar.
Sometimes courage is the quiet voice
at the end of the day saying, 'I will
try again tomorrow.'"

— Mary Anne Radmacher

8.

"It always seems impossible until it's
done."

— Nelson Mandela

9.

"Perseverance is the quiet hero that transforms dreams into reality."

— Anonymous

10.

"I am a slow walker, but I never walk back."

— Abraham Lincoln

11.

"If you're going through hell, keep going."

— Winston Churchill

12.

"Hardships often prepare ordinary people for an extraordinary destiny."

— C.S. Lewis

13.

"Perseverance, secret of all triumphs."

— Victor Hugo

14.

"Fall seven times, stand up eight."

— Japanese Proverb

15.

"The difference between a successful person and others is not a lack of strength, not a lack of knowledge, but rather a lack in will."

— Vince Lombardi

16.

"When the world says, 'Give up,' hope whispers, 'Try it one more time.'"

— Anonymous

17.

"In the confrontation between the stream and the rock, the stream always wins, not through strength but by perseverance."

— H. Jackson Brown Jr.

18.

"The only limit to our realization of tomorrow is our doubts of today."

— Franklin D. Roosevelt

19.

"Success seems to be largely a matter
of hanging on after others have let
go."

— William Feather

20.

"A river cuts through rock, not
because of its power, but because of
its persistence."

— James N. Watkins

21.

"Victory is always possible for the person who refuses to stop fighting."

— Napoleon Hill

22.

"The harder the conflict, the greater the triumph."

— George Washington

23.

"You may encounter many defeats,
but you must not be defeated."

— Maya Angelou

24.

"The road to success is dotted with
many tempting parking spaces."

— Will Rogers

25.

"What lies behind us and what lies before us are tiny matters compared to what lies within us."

— Ralph Waldo Emerson

26.

"Persistence can change failure into extraordinary achievement."

— Matt Biondi

27.

"You have power over your mind –
not outside events. Realize this, and
you will find strength."

— Marcus Aurelius

28.

"Most of the important things in the
world have been accomplished by
people who have kept on trying when
there seemed to be no hope at all."

— Dale Carnegie

29.

**"Don't be discouraged. It's often the
last key in the bunch that opens the
lock."**

— Anonymous

30.

"I will persist until I succeed."

— Og Mandino

31.

"Let me tell you the secret that has led me to my goal: my strength lies solely in my tenacity."

— Louis Pasteur

32.

"The best way out is always through."

— Robert Frost

33.

"Energy and persistence conquer all things."

— Benjamin Franklin

34.

"You just can't beat the person who won't give up."

— Babe Ruth

35.

"I've failed over and over and over again in my life and that is why I succeed."

— Michael Jordan

36.

"Failure is simply the opportunity to begin again, this time more intelligently."

— Henry Ford

37.

"It's not whether you get knocked
down, it's whether you get up."

— Vince Lombardi

38.

"Never confuse a single defeat with a
final defeat."

— F. Scott Fitzgerald

39.

"The greatest oak was once a little nut who held its ground."

— Unknown

40.

"Success is the sum of small efforts, repeated day in and day out."

— Robert Collier

41.

"You miss 100% of the shots you don't take."

— Wayne Gretzky

42.

"Don't watch the clock; do what it does. Keep going."

— Sam Levenson

43.

"A winner is just a loser who tried one more time."

— George M. Moore Jr.

44.

"Do not wait to strike till the iron is hot; but make it hot by striking."

— William Butler Yeats

45.

"Perseverance is the hard work you
do after you get tired of doing the
hard work you already did."

— Newt Gingrich

46.

"Great works are performed not by
strength, but by perseverance."

— Samuel Johnson

47.

**"Life is not about how fast you run
or how high you climb, but how well
you bounce."**

— Vivian Komori

48.

**"Difficulties mastered are
opportunities won."**

— Winston Churchill

49.

**"I think and think for months and
years. Ninety-nine times, the
conclusion is false. The hundredth
time I am right."**

— **Albert Einstein**

50.

**"Don't quit. Suffer now and live the
rest of your life as a champion."**

— **Muhammad Ali**

51.

"Patience and perseverance have a magical effect before which difficulties disappear and obstacles vanish."

— John Quincy Adams

52.

"Success is how high you bounce when you hit bottom."

— George S. Patton

53.

"Every strike brings me closer to the next home run."

— Babe Ruth

54.

"Difficulties in life are intended to make us better, not bitter."

— Dan Reeves

55.

"The man who moves a mountain begins by carrying away small stones."

— Confucius

56.

"Act as if what you do makes a difference. It does."

— William James

57.

**"Start where you are. Use what you
have. Do what you can."**

— Arthur Ashe

58.

**"Perseverance is not a long race; it is
many short races one after the other."**

— Walter Elliot

59.

"The difference between the impossible and the possible lies in a person's determination."

— Tommy Lasorda

60.

"Life is like riding a bicycle. To keep your balance, you must keep moving."

— Albert Einstein

Closing Reflection on Perseverance

Perseverance is not just an act of endurance, but an ongoing commitment to overcome. The quotes in this chapter are reminders that the strength to keep going lies within each of us. Challenges will arise, but those who persist—who continue to strive in the face of failure—are the ones who shape their own destinies. Every small step counts, and the only way to truly fail is to stop trying. Let these words guide you as you face the difficulties ahead, knowing that with perseverance, anything is possible.

2. LEADERSHIP AND VISION

Leadership is more than just giving orders or managing people; it's about inspiring others to dream bigger, work harder, and become better. True leaders possess the ability to see a future that others cannot yet envision, and they create a path to bring that vision to life. Leadership is the combination of guiding others with a sense of purpose while having the courage to take risks and face challenges head-on. It's about building trust, making decisions with integrity, and motivating people to work toward a common goal, even in uncertainty.

Vision, on the other hand, is what sets leaders apart from the rest. Vision is the art of seeing the invisible and believing in possibilities that have not yet been realized. The greatest leaders throughout history have not just been effective managers—they have been visionaries, people who saw a better future and inspired others to help them create it.

In this chapter, you'll discover 60 quotes from some of the world's greatest leaders, from political figures and business pioneers to cultural icons and revolutionary thinkers. Their words offer powerful insights into what it means to lead with vision, to inspire those around you, and to leave a lasting legacy.

61.

"The very essence of leadership is that you have to have a vision. It's got to be a vision you articulate clearly and forcefully on every occasion. You can't blow an uncertain trumpet."

— Reverend Theodore M. Hesburgh

62.

"Leadership is not about being in charge. It is about taking care of those in your charge."

— Simon Sinek

63.

"The greatest leader is not necessarily the one who does the greatest things. He is the one that gets the people to do the greatest things."

— Ronald Reagan

64.

"A leader is one who knows the way, goes the way, and shows the way."

— John C. Maxwell

65.

"Innovation distinguishes between a leader and a follower."

— Steve Jobs

66.

"Leadership is not about titles, positions, or flowcharts. It is about one life influencing another."

— John C. Maxwell

67.

"The function of leadership is to produce more leaders, not more followers."

— Ralph Nader

68.

"Where there is no vision, the people perish."

— King Solomon

69.

"Leadership is the capacity to translate vision into reality."

— Warren Bennis

70.

"A leader is best when people barely know he exists, when his work is done, his aim fulfilled, they will say: we did it ourselves."

— Lao Tzu

71.

"A good leader leads the people from above them. A great leader leads the people from within them."

— M.D. Arnold

72.

"The task of the leader is to get their people from where they are to where they have not been."

— Henry Kissinger

73.

"Leadership is the art of getting someone else to do something you want done because he wants to do it."

— Dwight D. Eisenhower

74.

"Before you are a leader, success is all about growing yourself. When you become a leader, success is all about growing others."

— Jack Welch

75.

"The best way to predict the future is to create it."

— Peter Drucker

76.

"To handle yourself, use your head; to handle others, use your heart."

— Eleanor Roosevelt

77.

"The very first step in achieving a goal is to have the right mindset. If you want to be a great leader, you have to think like one."

— Robin Sharma

78.

"Leadership is about making others better as a result of your presence and making sure that impact lasts in your absence."

— Sheryl Sandberg

79.

"Vision without action is merely a dream. Action without vision just passes the time. Vision with action can change the world."

— Joel A. Barker

80.

"A leader takes people where they want to go. A great leader takes people where they don't necessarily want to go, but ought to be."

— Rosalynn Carter

81.

"The best executive is the one who has sense enough to pick good men to do what he wants done, and self-restraint enough to keep from meddling with them while they do it."

— Theodore Roosevelt

82.

"I suppose leadership at one time meant muscles; but today it means getting along with people."

— Mahatma Gandhi

83.

"People ask the difference between a leader and a boss. The leader leads, and the boss drives."

— **Theodore Roosevelt**

84.

"Leadership is solving problems. The day soldiers stop bringing you their problems is the day you have stopped leading them."

— **Colin Powell**

85.

"The greatest leaders mobilize others by coalescing people around a shared vision."

— Ken Blanchard

86.

"Do not follow where the path may lead. Go instead where there is no path and leave a trail."

— Ralph Waldo Emerson

87.

"A genuine leader is not a searcher for consensus but a molder of consensus."

— Martin Luther King Jr.

88.

"Management is doing things right; leadership is doing the right things."

— Peter Drucker

89.

"Leadership is the ability to guide others without force into a direction or decision that leaves them still feeling empowered and accomplished."

— Lisa Cash Hanson

90.

"Don't find fault, find a remedy."

— Henry Ford

91.

"Outstanding leaders go out of their way to boost the self-esteem of their personnel. If people believe in themselves, it's amazing what they can accomplish."

— Sam Walton

92.

"Leadership is practiced not so much in words as in attitude and in actions."

— Harold S. Geneen

93.

"The challenge of leadership is to be strong, but not rude; be kind, but not weak; be bold, but not a bully; be thoughtful, but not lazy; be humble, but not timid; be proud, but not arrogant; have humor but without folly."

— Jim Rohn

94.

"Good leaders must first become good servants."

— Robert K. Greenleaf

95.

"Effective leadership is not about making speeches or being liked; leadership is defined by results not attributes."

— Peter Drucker

96.

"You don't lead by hitting people over the head—that's assault, not leadership."

— Dwight D. Eisenhower

97.

"The single biggest way to impact an organization is to focus on leadership development. There is almost no limit to the potential of an organization that recruits good people, raises them up as leaders, and continually develops them."

— John C. Maxwell

98.

"No man will make a great leader who wants to do it all himself, or to get all the credit for doing it."

— Andrew Carnegie

99.

"I have a dream that one day this nation will rise up and live out the true meaning of its creed: We hold these truths to be self-evident, that all men are created equal."

— Martin Luther King Jr.

100.

"A leader is someone who knows where they want to go, and gets there."

— James W. Johnson

101.

"I start with the premise that the function of leadership is to produce more leaders, not more followers."

— Ralph Nader

102.

"A leader is one who, out of the clutter, brings simplicity... out of discord, harmony... and out of difficulty, opportunity."

— Albert Einstein

103.

"Leadership and learning are indispensable to each other."

— **John F. Kennedy**

104.

"Do what you feel in your heart to be right—for you'll be criticized anyway."

— **Eleanor Roosevelt**

105.

**"The highest of distinctions is service
to others."**

— King George VI

106.

**"To add value to others, one must
first value others."**

— John C. Maxwell

107.

"The art of leadership is saying no, not yes. It is very easy to say yes."

— Tony Blair

108.

"The role of leadership is to transform the complex situation into small pieces and prioritize them."

— Carlos Ghosn

109.

"True leadership stems from individuality that is honestly and sometimes imperfectly expressed... Leaders should strive for authenticity over perfection."

— **Sheryl Sandberg**

110.

"The growth and development of people is the highest calling of leadership."

— **Harvey S. Firestone**

"Great leaders are not defined by the absence of weakness, but rather by the presence of clear strengths."

— John Zenger

"The function of leadership is to produce more leaders, not more followers."

— Ralph Nader

113.

"Whoever wants to be a leader among you must be your servant."

— Jesus Christ

114.

"In the end, leaders are not just about the results; they are about the journey."

— John C. Maxwell

115.

**"A leader is someone who
demonstrates what's possible."**

— **Mark Yarnell**

116.

**"You can't lead without the courage
to be yourself."**

— **Oprah Winfrey**

117.

"Effective leaders are not afraid to show their true selves."

— Simon Sinek

118.

"Leadership is about creating a culture where people can do their best work."

— Bill George

119.

"Every leader has the opportunity to turn every moment into a learning moment."

— John C. Maxwell

120.

"A leader is someone who knows where they want to go, and gets there."

— James W. Johnson

Closing Reflection on Leadership and Vision

Leadership and vision are intertwined in a powerful dance that shapes the future. The quotes in this chapter remind us that true leadership is not just about authority; it's about serving others, inspiring them, and creating an environment where everyone can thrive. As you reflect on these words, consider how you can embody the qualities of effective leadership in your own life. Whether you're leading a team, a project, or simply yourself, remember that your vision can inspire others to reach their potential. Embrace the power of leadership to create positive change, and let your vision light the way forward.

3. EMBRACING CHANGE AND INNOVATION

Change is the only constant in life. As we navigate through various stages of our personal and professional journeys, the ability to embrace change and foster innovation becomes paramount. In today's fast-paced world, where technological advancements and societal shifts occur at an unprecedented rate, adapting to change is no longer optional—it is essential for survival and success.

Innovation is the driving force behind progress, allowing us to find new solutions to old problems and envision possibilities that transcend the present. Embracing change and innovation requires a mindset open to learning, experimentation, and growth. It demands courage to step outside of comfort zones and the resilience to learn from failures.

This chapter compiles 60 quotes from influential thinkers, leaders, and innovators who have championed the importance of change and innovation. Their insights remind us that the willingness to adapt is a strength that leads to new opportunities and transformative growth. Let these words inspire you to embrace change, harness your creativity, and push the boundaries of what is possible.

121.

"Change is the law of life. And those who look only to the past or present are certain to miss the future."

— John F. Kennedy

122.

"Innovation is the lifeblood of progress, and embracing change is the key to unlocking its potential."

— Anonymous

123.

"The greatest danger in times of
turbulence is not the turbulence; it is
to act with yesterday's logic."

— Peter Drucker

124.

"Change is hard at first, messy in the
middle, and gorgeous at the end."

— Robin Sharma

125.

"The price of doing the same old thing is far higher than the price of change."

— Bill Clinton

126.

"To improve is to change; to be perfect is to change often."

— Winston Churchill

127.

"Every success story is a tale of constant adaption, revision, and change."

— Richard Branson

128.

"If you don't like change, you're going to like irrelevance even less."

— Ruth Simmons

129.

"The only way to make sense out of change is to plunge into it, move with it, and join the dance."

— Alan Watts

130.

"You can't change what you are, only what you do."

— Philip Pullman

131.

"Change before you have to."

— Jack Welch

132.

"If you want to make enemies, try to change something."

— Woodrow Wilson

133.

"The measure of intelligence is the ability to change."

— Albert Einstein

134.

"In a time of drastic change, it is the learners who will inherit the earth, while the learned will find themselves beautifully equipped to deal with a world that no longer exists."

— Eric Hoffer

135.

"Without change, there is no innovation, creativity, or incentive for improvement."

— William Pollard

136.

"To survive, a species must adapt to change."

— Charles Darwin

137.

"The ability to adapt is everything."

— Bob Parsons

138.

"Change is inevitable. Growth is optional."

— John C. Maxwell

139.

"Innovation is taking two things that are not yet together and putting them together in a new way."

— Tom Peters

140.

"It is not the strongest of the species that survive, nor the most intelligent, but the one most responsive to change."

— Charles Darwin

141.

"The secret of change is to focus all of your energy not on fighting the old, but on building the new."

— Socrates

142.

"You cannot control what happens to you, but you can control your attitude toward what happens to you."

— Brian Tracy

143.

"Change your thoughts and you change your world."

— Norman Vincent Peale

144.

"Every problem is a gift—without problems, we would not grow."

— Tony Robbins

145.

"The road to success is dotted with many tempting parking spaces."

— Will Rogers

146.

"The best way to predict the future is to create it."

— Peter Drucker

147.

"Innovation is the ability to see change as an opportunity—not a threat."

— Anonymous

148.

"Life is about how much you can take and keep fighting, how much you can suffer and keep moving forward."

— Anderson Silva

149.

"Success is not final, failure is not fatal: It is the courage to continue that counts."

— Winston Churchill

150.

"Adaptability is about the powerful difference between adapting to cope and adapting to win."

— Max McKeown

151.

"There is nothing permanent except change."

— Heraclitus

152.

"To be yourself in a world that is constantly trying to make you something else is the greatest accomplishment."

— Ralph Waldo Emerson

153.

"What we fear doing most is usually what we most need to do."

— Tim Ferriss

154.

"Innovation is not the product of logical thought, even though the final product is tied to a logical structure."

— Albert Einstein

155.

"It is not enough to be busy; so are the ants. The question is: What are we busy about?"

— Henry David Thoreau

156.

"It's not that we spend five days looking forward to just two. It's that most people do what they enjoy most on those two days. Those are the days they really live."

— James A. Murphy

157.

"The world is changing very fast. Big will not beat small anymore. It will be the fast beating the slow."

— Rupert Murdoch

158.

"Creativity is thinking up new things. Innovation is doing new things."

— Theodore Levitt

159.

"In every success story, you will find someone who made a courageous decision."

— Peter F. Drucker

160.

"Your life does not get better by chance, it gets better by change."

— Jim Rohn

161.

"The best thing you can do is the right thing. The next best thing is the wrong thing. The worst thing you can do is nothing."

— **Theodore Roosevelt**

162.

"People are not afraid of change; they are afraid of loss."

— **Anonymous**

163.

"The only thing that is constant is change."

— Heraclitus

164.

"Success is not just about what you accomplish in your life; it's about what you inspire others to do."

— Anonymous

165.

"Imagination is more important than knowledge. For knowledge is limited, whereas imagination embraces the entire world, stimulating progress, giving birth to evolution."

— Albert Einstein

166.

"Don't be afraid to give up the good to go for the great."

— John D. Rockefeller

167.

"If you do not change direction, you may end up where you are heading."

— Lao Tzu

168.

The future belongs to those who fearlessly embrace change and champion innovation as the driving force of human advancement."

— Confucius

169.

"Change is not a destination, just as
hope is not a strategy."

— Rudy Giuliani

170.

"Progress is impossible without
change, and those who cannot change
their minds cannot change
anything."

— George Bernard Shaw

171.

"Adaptability is the simple secret of survival."

— Jessica Hagedorn

172.

"The future belongs to those who believe in the beauty of their dreams."

— Eleanor Roosevelt

173.

"There is no innovation and creativity without failure. Period."

— Brene Brown

174.

"Change is the end result of all true learning."

— Leo Buscaglia

175.

"Innovation requires the courage to abandon certainties."

— Garry Hamel

176.

"You are never too old to set another goal or to dream a new dream."

— C.S. Lewis

"What we learn with pleasure we never forget."

— Alfred Mercier

"If you can dream it, you can do it."

— Walt Disney

179.

"Success is walking from failure to failure with no loss of enthusiasm."

— Winston Churchill

180.

"The man who moves a mountain begins by carrying away small stones."

— Confucius

Closing Reflection on Embracing Change and Innovation

Embracing change and fostering innovation is not just about survival; it's about thriving in an ever-evolving world. The quotes in this chapter inspire us to remain adaptable, challenge the status quo, and view change as an opportunity for growth. As you reflect on these words, think about how you can cultivate a mindset that welcomes change and nurtures innovation. Whether in your personal life, your career, or your community, remember that your willingness to adapt and innovate can lead to extraordinary outcomes. Let these insights guide you on your journey to becoming a catalyst for positive change.

4. COURAGE AND RESILIENCE

Courage and resilience are two of the most essential qualities one can cultivate in the face of life's challenges. They form the bedrock of personal strength, enabling us to navigate adversity, embrace change, and pursue our dreams. Courage is not the absence of fear; rather, it is the determination to act in spite of it. Resilience is the ability to bounce back from setbacks, adapt to difficult situations, and continue moving forward with renewed strength.

Throughout history, countless individuals have demonstrated remarkable courage and resilience, often in the face of overwhelming odds. Their stories inspire us to confront our fears and embrace challenges as opportunities for growth. Whether it's standing up for one's beliefs, overcoming personal hardships, or pursuing goals against all odds, the spirit of courage and resilience reminds us that we are capable of achieving greatness.

This chapter presents 60 quotes from influential figures who embody the essence of courage and resilience. Their words serve as powerful reminders that while challenges may be daunting, our inner strength can guide us through even the toughest of times. Let these insights inspire you to tap into your own courage and resilience, allowing you to face life's uncertainties with confidence and determination.

181.

**"Courage is not the absence of fear,
but the triumph over it."**

— Nelson Mandela

182.

**"It does not matter how slowly you
go as long as you do not stop."**

— Confucius

183.

"Courage is the compass that guides us through life's stormy seas, and resilience is the anchor that keeps us grounded."

— Anonymous

184.

"Our greatest weakness lies in giving up. The most certain way to succeed is always to try just one more time."

—— Thomas A. Edison

185.

"You may encounter many defeats, but you must not be defeated."

— Maya Angelou

186.

"The only limit to our realization of tomorrow will be our doubts of today."

— Franklin D. Roosevelt

187.

"Success is not final, failure is not fatal: It is the courage to continue that counts."

— Winston Churchill

188.

"The best way out is always through."

— Robert Frost

189.

"In the middle of difficulty lies opportunity."

— **Albert Einstein**

190.

"It is not the strongest of the species that survive, nor the most intelligent, but the one most responsive to change."

— **Charles Darwin**

191.

"Courage doesn't always roar.
Sometimes courage is the quiet voice
at the end of the day saying, 'I will
try again tomorrow.'"

— Mary Anne Radmacher

192.

"Resilience is accepting your new
reality, even if it's less good than the
one you had before."

— Elizabeth Edwards

193.

"What lies behind us and what lies before us are tiny matters compared to what lies within us."

— Ralph Waldo Emerson

194.

"Fall seven times, stand up eight."

— Japanese Proverb

195.

**"It's not whether you get knocked
down, it's whether you get up."**

— Vince Lombardi

196.

**"The only way to overcome a
challenge is to face it head-on, with
courage as your shield and resilience
as your sword."**

— Anonymous

197.

"You are never too old to set another goal or to dream a new dream."

— C.S. Lewis

198.

"The most common way people give up their power is by thinking they don't have any."

— Alice Walker

199.

"Keep your face always toward the sunshine—and shadows will fall behind you."

— Walt Whitman

200.

"The future belongs to those who believe in the beauty of their dreams."

— Eleanor Roosevelt

201.

"Hardships often prepare ordinary people for an extraordinary destiny."

— C.S. Lewis

202.

"Sometimes you don't realize your own strength until you come face to face with your greatest weakness."

— Susan Gale

203.

"Believe you can and you're halfway there."

— Theodore Roosevelt

204.

"Courage is grace under pressure."

— Ernest Hemingway

205.

"Out of difficulties grow miracles."

— **Jean de La Bruyère**

206.

**"Resilience is not just about how
much you can take before you break;
it's about how much you can take
after you break."**

— **Anonymous**

207.

**"You have power over your mind—
not outside events. Realize this, and
you will find strength."**

— Marcus Aurelius

208.

**"Challenges are what make life
interesting and overcoming them is
what makes life meaningful."**

— Joshua J. Marine

209.

"It always seems impossible until it's done."

— Nelson Mandela

210.

"Adversity does not build character; it reveals it."

— James Lane Allen

211.

**"You don't have to be great to start,
but you have to start to be great."**

— Zig Ziglar

212.

**"Strength does not come from
physical capacity. It comes from an
indomitable will."**

— Mahatma Gandhi

213.

"The struggle you're in today is developing the strength you need for tomorrow."

— Robert Tew

214.

"Courage is being scared to death but saddling up anyway."

— John Wayne

215.

"The most difficult thing is the decision to act; the rest is merely tenacity."

— Amelia Earhart

216.

"The only thing we have to fear is fear itself."

— Franklin D. Roosevelt

217.

"When you come out of the storm, you won't be the same person who walked in."

— Haruki Murakami

218.

"Everything you've ever wanted is on the other side of fear."

— George Addair

219.

"There is no failure except in no

longer trying."

— Elbert Hubbard

220.

"If you're going through hell, keep

going."

— Winston Churchill

221.

"Every adversity, every failure, every heartache carries with it the seed of an equal or greater benefit."

— Napoleon Hill

222.

"The greatest test of courage on earth is to bear defeat without losing heart."

— Robert Green Ingersoll

223.

"In the face of adversity, courage is the flame that ignites hope, and resilience is the fuel that keeps it burning bright."

— **Anonymous**

224.

"It's not the load that breaks you down; it's the way you carry it."

— **Lou Holtz**

225.

"Turn your wounds into wisdom."

— Oprah Winfrey

226.

"Sometimes you have to take a leap of faith first. The trust part comes later."

— Miriam L. MacGregor

227.

"The hardest thing to learn in life is which bridge to cross and which to burn."

— **David Russell**

228.

"Life doesn't get easier; you just get stronger."

— **Anonymous**

229.

"Strength is the product of struggle.
You must do what others don't to
achieve what others won't."

— Henry Rollins

230.

"Success is not measured by what
you accomplish but by the opposition
you have encountered."

— Orison Swett Marden

231.

"Courage is the power to let go of the familiar."

— Raymond Lindquist

232.

"You gain strength, courage, and confidence by every experience in which you really stop to look fear in the face."

— Eleanor Roosevelt

233.

"A hero is someone who has given his or her life to something bigger than oneself."

— Joseph Campbell

234.

"Resilience is the capacity to recover quickly from difficulties; toughness."

— Anonymous

235.

"Difficulties mastered are opportunities won."

— Winston Churchill

236.

"The best way to find yourself is to lose yourself in the service of others."

— Mahatma Gandhi

237.

"Pain is temporary. Quitting lasts forever."

— **Lance Armstrong**

238.

"If you stumble, make it part of the dance."

— **Anonymous**

239.

"Courage is like a muscle. We strengthen it by use."

— **Ruth Gordo**

240.

"What defines us is how well we rise after falling."

— **Lionel A. McLeod**

Closing Reflection on Courage and Resilience

Courage and resilience are not just traits; they are choices we make in the face of adversity. The quotes in this chapter remind us that while challenges are a natural part of life, it is our response to them that defines our journey. As you reflect on these words, consider the moments in your own life where you've had to summon courage or display resilience. Embrace the lessons learned from those experiences, and let them guide you in facing future challenges with confidence and strength. Remember, it is through adversity that we often discover our true selves and our greatest potential.

5. LOVE, KINDNESS, AND HUMANITY

Love, kindness, and humanity are the foundations of a fulfilling and meaningful life. These virtues connect us, inspire us, and propel us to act selflessly toward others. In a world that can often feel divided and chaotic, embracing love and kindness can create a ripple effect that fosters compassion, understanding, and harmony.

Throughout history, many great leaders, philosophers, and thinkers have emphasized the importance of love and kindness in building a better world. These values transcend cultural and geographical boundaries, reminding us that, at our core, we share a common humanity. By nurturing love and kindness in our daily lives, we can uplift ourselves and inspire those around us to do the same.

This chapter presents 60 quotes that highlight the significance of love, kindness, and humanity. Let these quotes inspire you to cultivate love and kindness in your interactions and recognize the profound impact that humanity can have in creating a more compassionate world.

241.

"Love your neighbor as yourself."

— Jesus Christ

242.

"Do to others as you would have them do to you."

— Jesus Christ

243.

"Let all that you do be done in love."

— **Apostle Paul**

244.

"The roots of all goodness lie in the soil of appreciation for goodness."

— **Dalai Lama**

245.

"Love one another. As I have loved you, so you must love one another."

— Jesus Christ

246.

"Father, forgive them, for they do not know what they are doing."

— Jesus Christ

247.

"Blessed are the merciful, for they will be shown mercy."

— Jesus Christ

248.

"By this everyone will know that you are my disciples, if you love one another."

— Jesus Christ

249.

"The greatest treasures are those invisible to the eye but found by the heart."

— Anonymous

250.

"Love is patient, love is kind."

— Apostle Paul

251.

"Kindness is the language which the deaf can hear and the blind can see."

— Mark Twain

252.

"No act of kindness, no matter how small, is ever wasted."

— Aesop

253.

"Where there is love, there is life."

— Mahatma Gandhi

254.

"The best way to find yourself is to lose yourself in the service of others."

— Mahatma Gandhi

255.

"Kindness begins with the understanding that we all struggle."

— Charles Glassman

256.

"The smallest act of kindness is worth more than the grandest intention."

— Oscar Wilde

257.

"Happiness is when what you think, what you say, and what you do are in harmony."

— Mahatma Gandhi

258.

"Love and compassion are necessities, not luxuries. Without them, humanity cannot survive."

— Dalai Lama

259.

"Let us always meet each other with a smile, for the smile is the beginning of love."

— Mother Teresa

260.

"We rise by lifting others."

— Robert Ingersoll

261.

"Love is composed of a single soul inhabiting two bodies."

— Aristotle

262.

"You can't blame gravity for falling in love."

— Albert Einstein

263.

"To love and be loved is to feel the sun from both sides."

— David Viscott

264.

"There is no remedy for love but to love more."

— Henry David Thoreau

265.

"A single act of kindness throws out roots in all directions, and the roots spring up and make new trees."

— Amelia Earhart

266.

"A friend loves at all times, and a brother is born for adversity."

— King Solomon

267.

"Love your enemies and pray for those who persecute you."

— Jesus Christ

268.

"Sometimes, the most productive thing you can do is relax."

— Mark Black

269.

"Kindness is a language which the deaf can hear and the blind can see."

— Mark Twain

270.

"Love is the beauty of the soul."

— Saint Augustine

271.

"For if you forgive other people when they sin against you, your heavenly Father will also forgive you."

— Matthew 6:14

272.

"Be kind and compassionate to one another, forgiving each other, just as in Christ God forgave you."

— Apostle Paul

273.

"The way to gain a good reputation is to endeavor to be what you desire to appear."

— **Socrates**

274.

"Act as if what you do makes a difference. It does."

— **William James**

275.

"The only way to do great work is to love what you do."

— Steve Jobs

276.

"The best thing to hold onto in life is each other."

— Audrey Hepburn

277.

"The greatest use of a life is to spend
it on something that will outlast it."

— William James

278.

"If you want to be a leader who
makes a lasting difference, show
others love and kindness."

— Anonymous

279.

"Nothing is more powerful than an act of kindness."

— Anonymous

280.

"We cannot all do great things, but we can do small things with great love."

— Mother Teresa

281.

"Love is the only force capable of transforming an enemy into a friend."

— Martin Luther King Jr.

282.

"Kindness is a mark of faith, and whoever is not kind has no faith."

— Muhammad

283.

"You cannot do a kindness too soon, for you never know how soon it will be too late."

— Ralph Waldo Emerson

284.

"Act with kindness, but do not expect gratitude."

— Confucius

285.

"To be kind is more important than to be right."

— Philippa Perry

286.

"In a world where you can be anything, be kind."

— Anonymous

287.

"A warm smile is the universal language of kindness."

— **William Arthur Ward**

288.

"The best way to cheer yourself is to try to cheer someone else up."

— **Mark Twain**

289.

"Wherever there is a human being, there is an opportunity for a kindness."

— Lucius Annaeus Seneca

290.

"It is not how much we have, but how much we enjoy, that makes happiness."

— Charles Spurgeon

291.

"Kindness is the sunshine in which virtue grows."

— Robert Green Ingersoll

292.

"Love is the greatest gift when given. It is the highest honor when received."

— James Cash Penney

293.

"To love oneself is the beginning of a lifelong romance."

— Oscar Wilde

294.

"The best thing to hold onto in life is each other."

— Audrey Hepburn

295.

"Love and kindness are never wasted. They always make a difference."

— Barbara De Angelis

296.

"When we give cheerfully and accept gratefully, everyone is blessed."

— Maya Angelou

297.

"The greatest gift of life is friendship, and I have received it."

— Hubert H. Humphrey

298.

"There is no exercise better for the heart than reaching down and lifting people up."

— John Holmes

299.

"No one has ever become poor by giving."

— **Anne Frank**

300.

"Love is a canvas furnished by nature and embroidered by imagination."

— **Voltaire**

Closing Reflection on Love, Kindness, and Humanity

In a world that often feels divided, overwhelmed by conflict and individual pursuits, the virtues of love, kindness, and humanity emerge as the threads that weave us together. These principles, ancient yet timeless, are not bound by culture, time, or place—they are the universal languages of the heart.

Love, in its many forms, is a force that propels us toward understanding and connection. It teaches us patience, empathy, and the courage to care even when it is difficult. Whether expressed through romantic relationships, familial bonds, or even simple acts of kindness between strangers, love forms the foundation upon which humanity thrives.

Kindness, a deliberate act of consideration for others, is an embodiment of our shared humanity. It is not restricted to grand gestures; instead, it flourishes in the small, everyday moments—a smile, a helping hand, a word of encouragement. In a fast-paced world, kindness reminds us to slow down and see one another for who we truly are, beyond our roles, achievements, or struggles.

Humanity, at its core, is the recognition of the common thread that binds all of us. It calls on us to be mindful of our collective experience, to support one another not just out of obligation but because we understand that in lifting others, we elevate ourselves. To be human is to see a reflection of ourselves in every face we encounter, to empathize with the joys and pains of others as though they were our own.

As we reflect on the stories and lessons in this chapter, it becomes clear that love, kindness, and humanity are not just ideals but practices—ones we must engage with daily. In doing so, we not only enrich our own lives but also contribute to a world that is more compassionate, more connected, and more just.

In the end, the greatest legacy we can leave behind is not material wealth or accolades, but the love and kindness we extend to others and the humanity we foster within ourselves.

6. SUCCESS AND GROWTH

Success and growth are intertwined concepts that inspire individuals to pursue their dreams and aspirations. Success is often seen as the culmination of hard work, determination, and resilience, while growth refers to the continuous journey of personal and professional development. Together, they form a powerful narrative that motivates us to reach our full potential.

Success is not solely measured by external achievements; it also encompasses the internal growth we experience along the way. Each setback, challenge, and victory contributes to our development, shaping our character and enhancing our understanding of ourselves and the world around us. Embracing growth means recognizing that learning is a lifelong process, and every experience, good or bad, provides us with valuable insights.

In this chapter, you will find 65 quotes that celebrate the themes of success and growth. These quotes, drawn from influential figures throughout history, will inspire you to take bold steps toward your goals and embrace the lessons that come from your journey. Let their wisdom guide you as you navigate the path to success and cultivate a mindset of growth.

301.

"Success is not final, failure is not fatal: It is the courage to continue that counts."

— Winston S. Churchill

302.

"The only limit to our realization of tomorrow will be our doubts of today."

— Franklin D. Roosevelt

303.

"Believe you can and you're halfway there."

— Theodore Roosevelt

304.

"Success usually comes to those who are too busy to be looking for it."

— Henry David Thoreau

305.

"The way to get started is to quit talking and begin doing."

— **Walt Disney**

306.

"Don't watch the clock; do what it does. Keep going."

— **Sam Levenson**

307.

"Success is walking from failure to failure with no loss of enthusiasm."

— Winston S. Churchill

308.

"I find that the harder I work, the more luck I seem to have."

— Thomas Jefferson

309.

"Success is not how high you have climbed, but how you make a positive difference to the world."

— Roy T. Bennett

310.

"Opportunities don't happen. You create them."

— Chris Grosser

$$311.$$

"You miss 100% of the shots you don't take."

— Wayne Gretzky

$$312.$$

"Success is not a destination, but a journey marked by continuous growth and unwavering determination."

— Anonymous

313.

"The future belongs to those who believe in the beauty of their dreams."

— Eleanor Roosevelt

314.

"What lies behind us and what lies before us are tiny matters compared to what lies within us."

— Ralph Waldo Emerson

315.

"Success is not in what you have, but who you are."

— Bo Bennett

316.

"The successful warrior is the average man, with laser-like focus."

— Bruce Lee

317.

"If you really look closely, most overnight successes took a long time."

— Steve Jobs

318.

"Your life does not get better by chance, it gets better by change."

— Jim Rohn

319.

"Success is to be measured not so much by the position that one has reached in life as by the obstacles which he has overcome."

— Booker T. Washington

320.

"Success is a journey, not a destination."

— Arthur Ashe

321.

"To succeed in life, you need three things: a wishbone, a backbone, and a funny bone."

— Reba McEntire

322.

"I never dreamed about success. I worked for it."

— Estée Lauder

323.

**"Success is getting what you want.
Happiness is wanting what you get."**

— Dale Carnegie

324.

**"The only place where success comes
before work is in the dictionary."**

— Vidal Sassoon

325.

"Success is not just about what you accomplish in your life; it's about what you inspire others to do."

— Anonymous

326.

"Hardships often prepare ordinary people for an extraordinary destiny."

— C.S. Lewis

327.

"In three words I can sum up everything I've learned about life: It goes on." -

— Robert Frost

328.

"Failure is the condiment that gives success its flavor."

— Truman Capote

329.

"Dream big and dare to fail."

— Norman Vaughan

330.

"You have to expect things of yourself before you can do them."

— Michael Jordan

331.

"The only real mistake is the one from which we learn nothing."

— Henry Ford

332.

"Success doesn't just find you. You have to go out and get it."

— Anonymous

333.

"If you want to achieve greatness, stop asking for permission."

— Anonymous

334.

"Success is a series of small wins."

— Anonymous

335.

"Perseverance is not a long race; it is many short races one after the other."

— Walter Elliot

336.

"Success is the result of preparation, hard work, and learning from failure."

— Colin Powell

337.

"The man who moves a mountain begins by carrying away small stones."

— Confucius

338.

"Your limitation—it's only your imagination."

— Anonymous

339.

**"Push yourself, because no one else is
going to do it for you."**

— Anonymous

340.

**"Great things never come from
comfort zones."**

— Anonymous

341.

"Dream it. Wish it. Do it."

— Anonymous

342.

"Success doesn't come from what you do occasionally; it comes from what you do consistently."

— Anonymous

343.

"If you want to succeed, you have to
let go of the past and stop being
afraid of what could go wrong."

— Anonymous

344.

"Success is not about the destination;
it's about the journey."

— Anonymous

345.

"The harder you work for something, the greater you'll feel when you achieve it."

— Anonymous

346.

"Don't be pushed around by the fears in your mind. Be led by the dreams in your heart."

— Roy T. Bennett

347.

"Sometimes we're tested not to show our weaknesses, but to discover our strengths."

— Anonymous

348.

"The only limit to our realization of tomorrow will be our doubts of today, so let's embrace challenges as opportunities for growth and success."

— George S. Patton

349.

"The best revenge is massive success."

— Frank Sinatra

350.

"Success is often the result of taking a misstep in the right direction."

— Al Bernstein

351.

"In the garden of life, success is the fruit of perseverance, nurtured by the seeds of hard work and watered by the rain of challenges."

— Anonymous

352.

"Doubt kills more dreams than failure ever will."

— Suzy Kassem

353.

"Opportunities multiply as they are seized."

— Sun Tzu

354.

"Success requires no explanations. Failure permits no alibis."

— Anonymous

355.

"What we fear doing most is usually what we most need to do."

— Tim Ferriss

356.

"Success is not in what you have, but who you are."

— Bo Bennett

357.

"The road to success and the road to failure are almost exactly the same."

— Colin R. Davis

358.

"Success is the ability to go from one failure to another with no loss of enthusiasm."

— Winston S. Churchill

359.

"The secret of success is to be ready when your opportunity comes."

— Benjamin Disraeli

360.

"Success means doing the best we can with what we have."

— Zig Ziglar

361.

"Your time is limited, so don't waste it living someone else's life."

— **Steve Jobs**

362.

"If you want to fly, give up everything that weighs you down."

— **Buddha**

363.

"Success is the progressive realization of a worthy goal."

— **Earl Nightingale**

364.

"Start where you are. Use what you have. Do what you can."

— **Arthur Ashe**

365.

"Success is the result of preparation, hard work, and learning from failure."

— Colin Powell

Closing Reflection on Success and Growth

Chapter 6, "Success and Growth," invites us to contemplate the intricate relationship between our aspirations and the journeys we undertake to achieve them. The quotes compiled in this chapter serve as powerful reminders that success is not merely a destination; it is a dynamic process shaped by our experiences, efforts, and resilience.

Reflecting on the quotes, we see a common thread: the importance of perseverance, adaptability, and a positive mindset. Many influential figures emphasize that setbacks are not failures but rather stepping stones toward growth. Each challenge we face can provide invaluable lessons, nudging us closer to our goals.

As you move forward in your own journey, consider what success means to you. Is it about recognition and accolades, or is it more about personal fulfillment and the impact you have on others?

Embrace the idea that growth comes from continuous learning, self-reflection, and an unwavering commitment to your dreams.

This chapter encourages you to take bold steps, seize opportunities, and cultivate a mindset that thrives on learning and improvement. Remember, the path to success is often paved with hard work, passion, and an unyielding belief in your potential. Let these reflections guide you as you navigate your own journey of success and growth, fostering not only personal achievements but also inspiring those around you.

CONCLUSION

HOW TO APPLY THIS WISDOM

As we reach the conclusion of "Voices of Inspiration," it's essential to reflect on how the wisdom shared throughout this book can be applied to our daily lives. Each quote represents not just words of encouragement, but also actionable insights that can guide our thoughts, behaviors, and interactions with others. Here are some ways to integrate this wisdom into your life:

1. **Cultivate a Growth Mindset**: Embrace challenges as opportunities for learning and personal development. Adopt the belief that your abilities and intelligence can be developed through dedication and hard work. This mindset will empower you to tackle obstacles with resilience.

2. **Practice Kindness and Compassion**: Small acts of kindness can have a profound impact on others and yourself. Strive to treat everyone you encounter with empathy and understanding. Remember that each person is facing their own battles, and a simple gesture can uplift someone's day.

3. **Set Clear Goals**: Inspired by the quotes on success, take time to define what success looks like for you. Set realistic, measurable goals that align with your values and aspirations. Break these goals into smaller, achievable steps, and celebrate each milestone along the way.

4. **Learn from Setbacks**: When faced with failure or adversity, view these moments as invaluable lessons rather than permanent defeats. Reflect on what went wrong, adjust your approach, and move forward with renewed determination.

5. **Surround Yourself with Inspiration**: Seek out positive influences in your life—be it books, podcasts, mentors, or friends who inspire you. Engage with individuals who uplift you and challenge you to grow. Their perspectives can provide fresh insights and keep you motivated.

6. **Reflect Regularly**: Make time for self-reflection to assess your progress, understand your emotions, and realign with your goals. Journaling your thoughts or meditating can help deepen this practice, allowing you to internalize the wisdom you encounter.

7. **Share the Wisdom**: Don't keep the inspiration to yourself. Share these quotes and insights with others, whether through conversations, social media, or community engagement. By spreading positivity and motivation, you contribute to a culture of encouragement and support.

8. **Stay Open to Change**: Embrace the idea that growth often comes from unexpected changes. Stay flexible in your plans and be willing to adapt as new opportunities arise. This openness will allow you to navigate life's complexities with grace and resilience.

In conclusion, the wisdom shared in "Voices of Inspiration" serves as a guiding light on your journey. By applying these insights in your daily life, you can cultivate a mindset that fosters success, embraces growth, and nurtures love and kindness. Remember that each day is a new opportunity to live out these principles and inspire others along the way. As you move forward, may you carry the voices of those who have come before you, and let their wisdom empower you to create a meaningful and impactful life.

IMPORTANT MATERIALS

The Bible: A timeless source of wisdom, guidance, and inspiration.

Affirmations for Children: The Makarios Way by Moses Feehi

A wonderful collection of affirmations aimed at helping children develop a strong sense of self-worth, faith, and resilience, all grounded in biblical principles.

Affirmations and Meditation for Students: The Makarios Way by Moses Feehi

A guide designed to empower students through affirmations and meditation, helping them build a strong foundation of faith, focus, and success.

Affirmations and Meditation for Business People: The Makarios Way by Moses Feehi

A powerful resource for business professionals, providing affirmations and meditations to inspire success, perseverance, and ethical leadership.

Affirmations for The Modern Men: The Makarios Way by Moses Feehi

A resource tailored to empower men with affirmations that promote strength, leadership, faith, and personal growth.

Affirmations for The Modern Woman: The Makarios Way by Moses Feehi

A guide specifically for women, offering affirmations that encourage confidence, grace, faith, and empowerment in every aspect of life.

How to Handle Personal Finances: The Makarios Way by Moses Feehi

This practical guide offers essential strategies for managing your finances wisely. Learn how to budget, save, and invest effectively while aligning your financial decisions with your values.

Tracking Your Finances: The Makarios Way by Moses Feehi

This resource provides tools and techniques for monitoring your financial health. Discover methods to track expenses, set financial goals, and maintain accountability, ensuring you stay on the path to financial success.

The Power of Your Mind by Pastor Chris Oyakhilome

This insightful book explores the incredible capabilities of your mind and how harnessing its power can lead to personal transformation and success

Rhapsody of Realities Daily Devotional by Pastor Chris Oyakhilome:

A wonderful tool to help young minds grow in faith, learn biblical principles, and apply them to everyday life.

Recreating Your World by Pastor Chris Oyakhilome

In this powerful work, Pastor Oyakhilome emphasizes the importance of aligning your thoughts with God's will to transform your life. Discover how to reshape your reality through faith, vision, and purpose.

Advice from an Old Man: The Makarios Way

A heartfelt collection of timeless insights aimed at helping readers face life's challenges with grace and purpose.

Prayer of Salvation

O Lord God, I come to you in the name of Jesus. Your word says whosoever shall call upon your name shall be saved. I believe with all my heart that Jesus is the Son of the Living God. I declare with my mouth that Jesus is the Lord of my life from this day. I declare that I am saved. I am a child of God. Amen.

www.ingramcontent.com/pod-product-compliance
Lightning Source LLC
Chambersburg PA
CBHW061036250726
48653CB00001B/114